EVENING
CHORE

The DreamSeeker
Poetry Series

Books in the DreamSeeker Poetry Series, intended to make available fine writing by Anabaptist-related poets, are published by Cascadia Publishing House under the DreamSeeker Books imprint and often copublished with Herald Press. Cascadia oversees content of these poetry collections in collaboration with DreamSeeker Poetry Series Editor Jean Janzen as well as in consultation with its Editorial Council and the authors themselves.

1. On the Cross
    By Dallas Wiebe, 2005
2. I Saw God Dancing
    By Cheryl Denise Miller, 2005
3. Evening Chore
    By Shari Wagner, 2005

Also worth noting are two poetry collections that would likely have been included in the series had it been in existence then:

1. Empty Room with Light
    By Ann Hostetler, 2002
2. A Liturgy for Stones
    By David Wright, 2003

EVENING CHORE

POEMS BY
SHARI WAGNER

DreamSeeker Poetry Series, Volume 3

DreamSeeker Books
TELFORD, PENNSYLVANIA

an imprint of
Cascadia Publishing House

Copublished with
Herald Press
Scottdale, Pennsylvania

Cascadia Publishing House orders, information, reprint permissions:
contact@CascadiaPublishingHouse.com
1-215-723-9125
126 Klingerman Road, Telford PA 18969
www.CascadiaPublishingHouse.com

Evening Chore

DreamSeeker Books is an imprint of Cascadia Publishing House
Copublished with Herald Press, Scottdale, PA
Library of Congress Catalog Number: 2004028812
ISBN: 1-931038-29-5
Book design by Cascadia Publishing House
Cover design by Gwen M. Stamm, based on painting by John Domont

See page 107 for details of
the grateful acknowledgements made to
John Domont for permission to use his painting as cover art; and
to the editors of the publications where many of these poems first appeared.

The paper used in this publication is recycled and meets the
minimum requirements of American National Standard for Information
Sciences—Permanence of Paper for Printed Library Materials, ANSI Z39.48-1984.1984

Library of Congress Cataloguing-in-Publication Data
Wagner, Shari, 1958-
Evening chore : poems / by Shari Wagner.
    p. cm. -- (DreamSeeker poetry series ; v. 3)
ISBN 1-931038-29-5 (trade pbk. : alk. paper)
I. Title. II. Series.
PS3623.A3564E94 2005
811'.6--dc22

                                                                    2004028812

12 11 10 09 08 07 06 05   10 9 8 7 6 5 4 3

For my husband, Chuck
And in memory of my grandfather, John Mishler,
who took me with him on his evening chore

In that singular light every little tree and shock of wheat, every sunflower stalk and clump of snow-on-the-mountain, drew itself up high and pointed; the very clods and furrows in the fields seemed to stand up sharply. I felt the old pull of the earth, the solemn magic that comes out of those fields at nightfall.

—Willa Cather

Contents

EVENING CHORE

Evening Chore

My grandfather has climbed into his truck,
a rusty blue ford with a few stray
bales of hay bouncing like children
in the back. He's riding out to the far
pasture where cows have been grazing
twenty-five years in the shade of some elms.
The dog that disappeared in a thunderstorm
and never came back is on the seat
beside him. He's making whiny noises
and thumping his tail like an amplified
heartbeat. Before the door falls shut
behind them, the old man is cupping his hands
to call the cows away from the shadows
and into the field where the last light is
already sinking.

A Cappella

As we gasp between lines
a chasm opens
from the older hymns.

I sense a darkness
like what I heard
at an Amish barn door,

the entrance to a church
or a cavern
where my ancestors

droned the poetry
that could not be uttered
in the village.

In sixteenth-century
dungeons
they sang these hymns

as a way to connect
flesh chained to walls
and racks. We hold

these broken ones
in our voices
like bread that could

bless us. Grandma Mishler,
whom we buried
the Easter when hyacinths

bloomed inside ice, leans
behind my left shoulder
and Shawn with the quick

laugh who died
giving birth
sits beside Grandfather

on the couch. They listen
with their eyes closed.
All of the old ones

are here in the dark
room of a house that
stood where corn grew

because God sent
the sun. We end with
"Praise God From Whom

All Blessings Flow"—
the version with echoing
alleluias and amens.

We don't need the book
and no one sets the pitch.
We've sung this one

at every marriage
and funeral. Even in-laws
with eyes on the last

five minutes of a game
join in from their corner.
From every direction

there are voices within
voices, husks beneath
husks. The dead sing

in a house so haunted
we breathe
the same breath.

Inheritance

They seem like another race
of women—these Mennonite wives
in the Mishler family album.
Sturdy as the chimneys
of old farmhouses, they turn
bundled infants toward
their bosoms, stare derisively
at cameras tilted below them.
If she were black, Great-Aunt Ida
could be a feminine Goliath
in a Clementine Hunter painting,
dwarfing the bearded brethren
on either side. We tremble
in the presence of Grandfather's
mother, a Wagnerian diva, who towers
above us on a porch, wearing
her covering like a horned helmet.
Rolled-up sleeves reveal
thick forearms, fists clench handles
of invisible buckets. "She was
a mild woman," says Aunt Doris.
"Are you kidding?" my mother
cuts in. "She carried
a switch and chased children
with it. I remember cleaning
her false teeth—thinking they
might bite." With milkshake diets
and jogging, we've tried to
exorcise them from our bodies—
to expel Holstein hips and legs
stout as Belgian horses. But
even when we starve ourselves

into weakness, the inheritance
remains like a curse that can't
be lifted or the framework
of a barn that bows to nothing
but the gravity that would claim it.

The Farm Wife Ruminates on Cows

If I'd been born a fortune teller,
I'd read my family's future
in black peninsulas of Holsteins. I'd see
my grandmother, an orphan growing up,
rub her hands on December mornings
in steam where they had lain.

The only dream my mother ever told
was how she drew away the baby quilt
and saw the snout, the full-moon eyes.
Pregnant, I would dream of joining them
in the fields, our bodies, heavy pears, pulling
branches to the ground.

My girls believe they're named for Bible women
but each was named for a favorite cow,
a blessing of sorts, the only kind I knew, so that
even if they never have cattle in their barns
or live near fields in which they graze
they will have one guardian with a steadfast shape.

The Farm Wife Sells Her Cows

The cats gather by my kitchen door,
rubbing ribs against a box of overshoes
and spewing curses that waver
like an organ's vibrato. I've given them
every left-over in the fridge—none of it
seems to soothe them, though when we enter
the dairy room where a sour scent still lingers
they hush and assume places, calico
sphinxes against the wall.

I switch on the radio, wait for
the first ones to lumber through—black
and white boulders—larger than you'd imagine
watching them in the field. If only
we could call them back, but by now
they must be past the beltway of Indianapolis,
peering through slats with eyes bewildered
as on the day we pulled them from their mothers.

The Blessing

For the space of four hours,
from Indianapolis to my grandparents'
farm near Shipshewana,
my father and I plowed
past dark fields, singing:
      "Vegetables grow
in my garden, God sends the rain.
Vegetables grow in my garden,
God sends the sun."
                With each verse
we substituted something new:
corn-on-the-cob, strawberries,
zucchini, coconuts. The trick,
never stop for breath.

I did not know we carried
my stillborn brother
in that car
        and that his blessing
would be a song that twisted
around and around, clinging
to this world like a vine.

Rook

The rook was the first
bird I recognized. Garbed
in black, it resembled
my great-grandmother who
warned against vanity
and the worldliness of face
cards with their kings, queens,
and jacks. Good Mennonites
chose rook instead of pinochle
or poker. Perched upon
a lap, I learned my colors
from the cards and pondered
the ambiguity of words—
how someone could lose
a hand or look inside a kitty.
My father could con you
into going set with his
physician's face but my mother
and her family of farmers
would forecast their failures.
"Oh, gussy," Aunt Doris would
groan. "I don't have anything
above a twelve." Even
their battered cards revealed
where the bird had come
to roost. When I turned thirteen,
we packed the deck and moved
to the Horn of Africa where
missionaries hunched around
kerosene lanterns to play
rook low with a double deck.
I could sense concentric circles

surrounding our table—
the compound, the village,
the desert, the ocean.
The encyclopedia said our bird
was omnivorous like marabou
storks, those stately old
gentlemen who stood statuesque
in the garden but in a lunatic rush
devoured left-over scraps. Back
in Indiana, the game for pacifists
became a war between the sexes.
Young men began the bid
at 140 and dared to shoot
the moon while their opponents
watched each other's faces
to deduce when to "check"
or "pass" and which trump
to call. Normally, I couldn't
speak to boys, but at my cousin's
church parties, as I arranged
my fan of cards, the bird
whispered the words to say.
Years later, my fiancé taught me
poker and I schooled him
in the rudiments of rook before
introducing him to my parents.
He found it strange that when
the dead hand was my partner
the bird would nest inside
the stack and when we traveled
rooks seemed to follow us
like Woden's ravens, Memory
and Thought. When Grandpa forgot
the trump color and values

of cards, we substituted Uno
until Alzheimer's stole even
that away. Since then, we keep
our decks inside a drawer.
The men stretch out to watch
sports on cable while women
congregate in the kitchen to talk
about children and exchange
photographs. Our new games
are always changing and it takes
time just to learn the rules.
Last Christmas at Doris' house,
we shook tiny pigs whose flanks
we read like dice and on my
father's side we played a game
of '60's music with lyrics only
my husband knew. As my uncle
ruminated upon the second line
of "Suspicious Minds," our blackbird
scratched his angry talons
against the box of Trivial Pursuit.

Second Language

On their ankles and arms girls wore
leather bracelets with oily lockets
sewn shut like their virginity.
My father who took out stitches said
they carried them for a charm to ward off
demons and disease, serpents that slept
in the same fields. You would find
if you cut them open, pages from
a holy book with print too small to read.
I wondered how they knew the words
were in there. This was the year

I turned thirteen, began pecking out
poetry on a manual typewriter with sticky
keys that left smudges around the letters.
I wanted to describe large, empty places,
the desert where Somali nomads carried
their houses. As they walked they composed
in an unwritten language lyrics
that traveled in circles like the wind
or the voice of the young muezzin
calling from the minaret of the mosque.
Even in my bedroom his notes rippled
through darkness growing larger.

I never learned the language, but
later rustling corn leaves spoke
a tongue I hadn't heard before and carved
deep in the skin of beech were cryptic
poems I could partially decipher,
words of love or loss we carry
within us, our amulets, our houses,
as we travel through desolate spaces.

The Compound

Jamama, Somalia

The generator buzzes like some
giant cicada and the compound
of green cement houses surrounded
by barbed wire fence springs
into light. My mother plugs
in the iron. I reach for a book.

Later, we play Clue and as I guess
"Professor Plum in the Billiard Room
with a Lead Pipe," the lights blink
a warning to dash for lanterns—
too late. My sister and I fumble
for shoes, feeling the scuttle
of scorpions in the dark. Anything
could crawl through cracks stuffed
with Kleenex and tape so we check
sheets, poke beneath beds. One night

a nurse awoke to the clatter
of aluminum falling. Above the stove,
something nudged pans with a triangular
head. His body, in the beam
of her light, flowed like thick syrup—
the Sacred Python that coursed
through my book. Villagers let him enter
their houses, sip from their gourds.

The nurse gave him a swat
with her broom. Inscrutable
as the face of a shadow, he slid
out the door, a length of old rope
trailing its anchor.

Family Tree
Kenya, 1972

Mr. Planck draws a triangle on the board—
Father, Son, Holy Ghost—and boxes bearing
a bloodline to the cross.
                          In the distance coffee workers
gather beans in baskets, their shirts and dresses
blossoming like bougainvillea while he describes
how "Allah" is another name for God. I ponder
pilgrims kneeling toward a huge black cube
and kissing Gabriel's gift, the fragment
of a fallen star, inside. I draw Kaabas
in the margins of my notebook, Kaabas stacked
on Kaabas.
            All we have left
is two weeks for African Tribal Religion. Outside,
coffee fields are empty, but near the tennis court,
our dorm-father builds a tripod for his telescope.
The Bantu believe God moves like wind, just above the forest,
and when people die, their spirits roost in ancestral branches,
villagers bring them food.
                          My notes sprout curly-headed
baobabs; God in the shape of a cloud, bounces
above the leaves and people are little x's, alive or dead, who slip
in and out of circles, rings inside a tree.

The Dog that Disappeared in a Storm
And Never Came Back

is the dog my grandfather calls
while he lies immobile, afraid
to shift the soft chalk

of his bones. Thunder shook
the cucumber fields the night
he stood in the cold rain

calling, but the dog never
came and they never found
his burnt body though they searched

the fields and soft-needled woods.
He reaches for the ribbon snake
he stashed as a child by his bed—

it still amazes him
how the snake must have escaped
like water slipping through

the meshed wire lid.
Across wet fields,
the abandoned house stands

surrounded by spirea bushes
where catbirds sang
in the morning and he and Henry

played cops and robbers
in the tall, empty rooms.
Once when they heard a sound

like footsteps on the stairs, Henry
leaped from the second story,
landing on his feet, motioning

his brother to follow. My grandfather
raises the hand we are holding
together and I know he is ready

to step out the window
where now it's so dark
the catbirds are quiet.

His Silence

was a table of empty glasses
his daughters rushed to fill.
It was a shadow collecting
near their feet, a patch of dirt
they could never sweep away.
Behind his back they dubbed him
"Silent Sam" and backed away
as if the space around him were
something oppressive and dead,
a bear skin rug in summer.

It was not until he died
that they forgave his silence.
Each year it calls them
with the persistence of killdeer
to the clearing in Michigan—
the remains of a root cellar
and chimney-stones lodged in dirt.

Three abreast they walk a fire line,
the road he traveled alone
each morning through pine trees
that in winter's darkness
must have creaked like stairways
of old houses. His daughters want

to hold that boy who walks
before them, toting a gunny sack
of books and fingering buckeyes
he carries as charms against foes.

They want to nuzzle him with
the reassurance of their faces
before he reaches the wrought-iron
gate and it swings shut
behind him with the cold
precision of words.

II

At Dawn in the Subdivision

A heron, stoic as a statue, is gazing
downward as if golden fish
hovered near lilies
or just his own reflection
held fast to the still surface
of the retention pond.

What has drawn him to this side
of the looking-glass, where
stands of cattails are branded
as outlaws and grass is the shade
of artificial turf even in winter?
This is the summer the tadpoles
never transform into frogs.
Only one lone voice calls
and hesitates before dialing
the same number again.
At night we close our window—the length
of his silence and of his patience
keeps us awake.

Now we stand at the same window
stunned by the heron's poised
beauty and waiting for great wings
to shake the air
loose from its moorings,
but the first moment we turn, he is
gone as if never here.

And it is good he is gone.

I wish him rivers of fish untainted
by run-off from lawns too lethal
for my daughter to touch in bare feet,
lawns where twelve glassy-eyed ducks
lay iridescent as gasoline. The foxes
with cubs come no more
and neither should you, O heron,
with the placid, unblinking eye.

Go back before you become an ornament
in some anonymous lawn, a tribute
to those remembered in death. Yes,
go back where you came from, to waterways
lush with tadpoles and others of your tribe.

The Lighthouse Keeper's Wife

My husband, as a child in bed, watched
the lighthouse—lit by an orange bulb
from some old string of Christmas
lights—and imagined himself a miniature
man, climbing the tiny steps, slippery
from the spray, chiseled
in a rock slab base. Then he'd enter
the door, arched like a cathedral
entrance. He told me this

on our wedding night, on the balcony
of the Getaway Motel in Indianapolis,
as we stared, below us, at stammering
neon lights. A year later
we moved to the Atlantic Coast
and he found a job as lighthouse keeper.
Year after year, he climbed the spiral
staircase while I followed. At first,
I imagined ships were coming and squinted
toward the ocean's edge. One had purple
sails and a cargo of parakeets, violin
music that cried like a human voice.

But never was I lonely, though for days
we saw no one but ourselves and both of us
started collecting things: scallop shells,
broken coral, pieces of bottle glass
rubbed into polished stones. Looking through them
was like peering through stained glass windows, only
these were a softer shade. Not everything

was easy. Once, when my husband left for town,
the fog bell broke, and I pulled for hours on strands
of unbraided rope, once every fifteen seconds, until
my blistered palms broke open. Several times
the wind blew small boats against our shore
and we stumbled through icy, frothy waves to catch
their sides and lead them in. What we noticed first

was how our hands were getting smaller
in relation to the fish and how the waves were growing,
curling higher, more exuberantly, like the sky
in a Van Gogh painting. The light from our windows
was another clue: it shone so slim upon the water,
the shape of electric eels. After half a century,

the Coast Guard installed a computerized light and fog bell.
They scooped us up, like fish in a plastic bag,
and drove us to a Home in Indianapolis.
But we had become too small to fit the human world.
My husband couldn't reach the door knob, and even stretching
I wasn't tall enough to see, above the window ledge, the buildings
clouding the horizon.

The day my husband died, I climbed
into the lighthouse we kept beside our bed. I've bolted
all the windows and warm my hands—the blood veins branching
like violet sea fans—over the electric flame.

The Gathering

We stop, not for the pedestrian light,
but to watch the courthouse tree,
its winter branches quivering with wings
like dried leaves, thousands and thousands.
As if a gust of wind lifts them
they rise, one cloud, into the heavy sky.
They swing, like skaters playing crack-the-whip,
three times around the courthouse square
strung with silver lights, then divide
over and over like amoebae and swim
behind the Episcopal Church.

While they are gone and we stand looking
upward, as if for fireworks, a man
emerges from a parked car, joins our corner.
"I almost hit someone, watching
the birds—starlings," he says.

Suddenly, they are back, wheeling
above our heads, a spiraling molecule
of DNA. We remember the news
on public radio, only the night before,
how dinosaurs were more like birds
than lizards—warm-blooded,
traveling in herds. Imagine,
you say, how this must have looked
when birds were dinosaurs.

And now their flight becomes
some ancient calligraphy I've forgotten
how to read. When the birds finally settle
and resume the shape of leaves, the sky seems

so deserted, like a child's magic stencil board
when the page has been lifted
and the writing disappears.

The Birders of Cool Creek Park

Come snow-glare or storm-light,
come swaths of gold to shift
through leaves, come mist to cleave
to mud, these Saturday morning
pilgrims keep to trails hemmed
by Wal-mart and Discount
Tires. Through traffic drone
they discern the chirp of a yellow-
rumped warbler and a solitary
vireo's snippet of song. The hint
of a hermit thrush, a few flute-like
trills, pulls them into a quiescent hush
until the white-throated sparrow
quickens the air. They speak
of children balancing jobs,
a flooded basement, a home
on the market, yet they perceive
high in the sycamore, an oriole's
faint flicker. "Find ten o'clock
in that small tree," they say, patiently
pointing me to the ruby-crowned kinglet
in all that densely dappled green.
When I find him, it's like opening
the tab on an advent calendar,
the distinctive eye-ring and hidden
crown, modest herald of a forgotten
world where red-berried bushes
are beaded with the day's first light.

If It's Bones You Want,

a piece by piece wired resurrection in the atrium of a museum,
a royal gawkiness bordered by a braided rope with tassels,
then you'll need your pick and shovel,
wagons and mules, shoe boxes for separating pieces,
plenty of light, masking tape, indelible ink.
Each fragile fossil you must handle between your fingers.

But if, on the other hand, it's the real thing you're after,
all you will need is a good length of rope
and, beyond that, steady nerve
as you lower yourself into the sinkhole,
down through a cave-pit opening, rappelling yourself past
layers of mossy, stratified rock, white and pink anemones,
a static waterfall, into the gape of darkness
where brown bats cluster against the walls,
the bell-shaped chamber—
finally, the floor.

Then to choose your tunnel, chimney through spaces
you'd think had no footholds, catch your breath
in a room of formations: stalagmites and stalactites,
a maze of incisors. You must watch your head;
calcified curtains may shatter. In clear, pebbled streams,
blind fish, always just beyond your grasp, quiver.
The circle from your carbide light grows dimmer,
you smell the grittiness of oxide. Whenever you cock your head,
water from your light escapes.

Somewhere ahead of you and below,
a primordial form rises from the lake.
It will be listening for your footsteps,
has been listening

as you push your way through the narrowest of tunnels,
moving on your stomach, headfirst.
You think you hear it breathing,
and then the sudden room—
a drop of sixty feet,
a ceiling of a hundred.

What you sense is a presence
beneath you, a bulk.
Your flickering light will reveal the briefest of glimpses:
a head, a slope of neck.

Then the heavy descending of a body,
a boulder, an anchor dropping,
taking with it an entire length of rope.
It has gone deeper,
will always go deeper,
will always be more submerged than exposed,
in every encounter more than you can handle.

Carp

The Japanese called them
swimming flowers,
these fish
half-hidden
beneath pavilions
of floating leaves.

At first I catch
only glimpses: a petal
of creamy orchid,
a sleeve
of orange silk.

Cupping
my hands just
slightly,
I try a trick
I've used with catfish,
clap a constant
and reverberating
thunder.

A carp
zigzags
out of a cloud
of leaves, lured
by curiosity
or the familiar
pulse
of her own heart.

She shimmers
like sherbet
melting in the sun
and trails
what I imagine
is a koi's invisible
kite string
of Chinese blessings:
Good Fortune,
Strength,
Long Life.

On and on
the fish keeps
gliding
and not until she
enters that dark
continent
of my shadow
do I consider
stopping
the ancient drumbeat,
half-afraid she might,
as legends claim,
walk upright
upon the shore.

But the carp veers
of her own accord,
back beneath
the brown and green
tapestry
of willow.

I know the hunger
of those who swallow
the flaming bodies,
alive and slippery—
a desire to feel
within their own
cave river
a presence
brilliant and breathing.

I search my pockets,
toss silver coins
I wish were bread.

Cork Carving

Old men going blind
carve landscapes
out of cork. Anywhere
they look afterwards,
shadows like those upon
the latticework
of this Chinese pavilion
appear in a haloed border
as if small lanterns
were lit at the base.

But no one is moving inside—
not even a servant
in blue slippers,
though the roof holds
itself up like a curtsy
and ornamental trees
pedestal their leaves
like china cups
they are careful
never to drop.

In the river
beside the pavilion,
two egrets balance
on palmetto islands.
The smaller is watching
fish swim invisible water
while the other
with head held alert
hears a sound in the distance,
footsteps of old men

who circle the thicket
searching for a footpath
before it is dark
and their lanterns
grow dim.

Sea Turtles

       If they were free
they could lead us to an underwater
kingdom where seasons are kept
behind rice paper screens. Break them
and blossoms blown to our feet
swirl in eddies of snow.
                    Or perhaps
they would take us to a sarcophagus shell.
What if, like statues of saints that open to reveal
the story of their torture, the sea turtle split
along her line of longitude?
                    Inside
would be a cavern and the only sound,
the echo of the sea.

Little One
To Vienna

I listen to your swift
heartbeat breaking
ocean static and picture
your translucent skin
blinking gills.

I am seasick
for love of you
my slippery tadpole
my sleepy lizard
my parakeet fluttering
against the ribs
of its cage.

When you gasp
your first sharp breath
the light will be
a kind of blindness
but I will hold you
in the boat of my arms

and when you have forgotten
the language of water
I will tell you
as my mother told me
old fairy tales
of swans who shed
their feathered jackets
on the beach

and stories of what swims
beneath our keel—
those creatures we have been
who remember us
and guide us
when we've lost all sight of land.

III

Covered Bridge

The same space still spans the river
though there are no creaking boards
to cross, no passage through something

basking in the sun. Near its mouth
we filled plates with barbecued
chicken and 7-up salad and when

we drove home, lovers who left
bottles, dark and sour, moved closer
into the dusk. Even on humid afternoons,

it was cooler by this placid curve
of the Wabash, shaded by ash
and fields away from where things

stirred. Only the undulation of water
was real, and when I peered through
the floor, where did it go, that gap

between surface and bridge?
The old ones recall how when sunlight
struck at just the right angle, the past

reappeared: *Red Front Drug Store*
and *Herron's Barber Shop,* placards
interspersed with the inevitable

initials of lovers plighting
their troth. Girls in white frocks
who planted easels on the bank

still paint from memory the vivid
blush of the bridge and feel, as they dip,
the river's cold edge, the distance

from where they stood and the stockings
sloughed on the rocks.

The Isle of Iona
To Iona Colleen

Go in the drizzle, alone
or with someone so close
silence shifts its weight
like a backpack.

In the shadow
of the Celtic Cross,
feel the rocks beneath your feet—
they were holy
even before St. Columba
claimed them for Christ.

Rest in the clover that blankets
what might have been
an altar where a young woman
prayed to forget the arms
that would never hold her.
Eight hundred years ago
she crossed the same gray water
to reach these walls you touch
and time recedes behind you.

In the abbey church, pilgrims
in T-shirts read the liturgy
while you listen for the vibrations
of a voice still wavering
in the air.

Iona will rise
as the waters rise.

When the Second Flood comes,
the kings of Scotland will sleep
undisturbed beneath stones
rubbed blank by a thousand years
of rain. The harpist on the street
lays down his black case and sings,

"Will ye go, lassie, go?
And we'll all go together. . . ."

Mahalia

She is the only one left
to learn the designs. When she loses

the pattern, no going back, instead
a new basket that gathers

and blooms, a gourd holding
darkness. In the shade

of crepe myrtle, her mother splits
cane and tells stories:

Uncle Columbus in Chicago
who marked his way to the factory

with pieces of chalk; the unfinished
basket that swallowed

the weaver; and the girls
who wore jeans, married soldiers,

never came back. Mahalia takes her machete
into the cane brake where feathers of light

fall on her shoulders and a single leaf
shakes without wind—a sign

that the old ones are watching
as they move through.

Amish Farm with Girl
With quotations from "The Red Wheelbarrow"
by William Carlos Williams

so much depends
upon
seven hundred brown and white
pullets running through tall
grass and your bare feet, your
face splashed by light
as if you had dived
under the rush of the pump
and come up for breath
in love with the world, every
inch of five acres, the elm
with its rope swing grazing
the sky, fields tilting
in every direction. The dirt
is alive. Nothing will deter it
from raising its brood
of petals and thistles, and you
wouldn't say it in so many words
but you know nothing makes sense
by itself, but by how it crosses
a path or slants toward a roof.

So much depends then
upon
the corn *glazed*
with rain and a girl
in a plain blue dress
a few shades bolder
than the sky.

The House of the Deaf Woman
and the Belfry at Eragny
1886 / Camille Pissarro
Indianapolis Museum of Art

Beneath a spindly tree,
the woman in Pissarro's orchard

kneels in her own blue-green
shadow, gathering fallen

apples or flecks of sunlight
reflected in the grass. Nothing

will ever fill her bushel basket
for nothing is solid here—not

the walnut's stippled trunk
nor the steeple clad in motes

of slate. If bells could peal
the hour, still, the sound

would falter, muffled by clouds
banking the roofline's dappled glint.

Half-hidden by branches, the deaf woman's
brick house shimmers like grass,

like leaves, like everything ephemeral
caught in summer's morning sun. Only

a small doorway and the attic dormer
pronounce some dark density

of interior space that holds
the eye and leads it back

to a shadow in the foreground
detached from the apple tree

Pissarro stood by, the same one
which in our deaf state

we pause near, sensing its
absence and the dissolution

of order, the hard sting
of nettles sprung from where

the figure in a straw hat kneels,
her back turned toward us.

The Garden

A slow rain revives the dusty miller
and the yellow coreopsis that fell

like hair brushed forward
across the stone path. Listen,

the garden is singing. From its
green throat swells a ballad, how a man

wed the spirit of a tree disguised
as a woman. This story inevitably ends

in disaster for the man. The woman stiffens
into the bark of a tree just as the swan-wife

shakes loose from the fisherman's
hearth. Remember the moon's daughter

who climbed down a ladder
of knotted silk? The farmer and his child

will never touch her luminous face
though they wait all night in a silent field.

*In this life nothing remains but the memory
of loss.* This is the song the garden sings and yet

it is not sad. Coming and going, a traveler
drifting between darkness and light, the garden

knows better than anyone that the story of what
it loses is the story of what it loves.

Persephone

What if you had never reached
for that forbidden flame—
the narcissus near your feet?
Would the earth have stayed
the same? Or, having seen
what you dared not touch
would the morning's dew
have crystallized to snow? Because

you turned toward your desire
even the earth beneath you broke.
Horses breathing fire rushed
from inside the dark. His arm
around your waist. The frenzy—
not knowing what could happen.
So many gates to pass through,
circles spiraling downward.

In a foreign country, your mother
rubbed her face with cinders,
the leaves flared red and withered.

No more idle days, twisting clover,
nights in hollow trees.
Although the door was heavy,
the moving between worlds
gave you the power
to stir the dogwood blossom
and call the herons home.

Psyche

Happily—yes—but not for ever after,
not in such an insubstantial home,
each day the light rubbing away pillars,
the foundation vanishing into a flock
of nasturtiums, trilliums and bellworts.
A shaft of amber instead of the kitchen table,
ash leaves in the same room where I loosened
my hair, the place I slept an exuberance
of fern. If I clapped my hands, no one
moved to meet me, no sound but the river.

Even if I never raised the candle,
the honeymoon could not have lasted.
The question of who we really were
would have assumed the shape of a beast
crouched at the window.

Now I journey over and under this earth,
collecting pieces of myself. I am learning
to believe the voices, to gather my strength
from the ants, eagle, reeds, even stones.

This secret box, Persephone's from the underworld,
the one I dare not open, see, I lift the lid.

The Miller's Wife

My husband tended the wheel that made
the flour I sold by loaves in the street.
No one knew our names. We were
as plain as the gray stones left by glaciers
that I gathered for a pathway
through my garden, and our cottage
was the smallest, bordered on one side
by the stream, on the others by the forest
that at night sent spirits of animals
our hands fashioned on dimly-lit walls.
It must have been one of these
who granted our wish, gave us a child
so beautiful at birth that we gasped.

Soon villagers in the market drew near
just to gaze upon her. From the most remote
regions of the kingdom, peasants arrived,
imploring with arthritic fingers
which in my worst moments resembled
baited hooks. When the queen felt the flesh
on her heels hardening into hooves,
she iced the tarts with arsenic to harbor
in the deepfreeze.

My daughter, dressed in yellow and glowing
among the daffodils, is sunshine spun
from straw. I am her second shadow—closer
than her own—but there are so many dangers.
Even the stream that turns our mill
hums a lullaby and flashes its silver
just beyond her reach. There is little time
to teach her the riddles I never had to use.

Already at the edge of dreams I hear
a horse and rider stumble over rocks, catch
themselves in brambles. We practice
in the willow's shade:

If he asks you to spin a hundred jackets
smaller than a thimble, ask him to build
the loom. If he tells you to come neither
on foot nor on horseback, saddle
a nanny goat. Remember, the swiftest of all
is the wind, the fattest is the earth
for it feeds us, the softest, the hand
that cradles the head resting
on eiderdown. Nothing in the world
is lovelier than sleep.

They would keep you in a gilded tower
with no windows and a hairbrush. So

don't let them catch you. Be as clever
as water that guides small boats
past our mill, vanishes
into air and swells into clouds
that hover above
the head of the queen.

The Farmer's Wife

Behind those peaceful scenes
devised for inland folk
who must have beauty anchored down,
the ocean I imagine
rolls like a windy cornfield,
tossing tassels and dark green leaves.
It could take my breath
and never bring it home again.

When asked if I would marry,
I said, to the chagrin of my family,
that he would have to be a sailor,
a man who moved lightly across the water,
setting sails by constellations.
But after years I grew tired
waiting in the fields.
For a time I dressed in black
and then put on my white.

When all the vows were said and done,
I discovered what I never looked to see:
I had married a man who counted
his fortune by the number of bushels,
by the starlings he shot from the rafters.

For every machine he buys,
I buy another tree,
a quaking aspen,
to grow in the circle
reaching around my house.
Whenever a gale comes from the North,
I stand against the kitchen screen
and hear the leaves
like rising water.

Diana of the Dunes

*"Over the years, more than one person has reported seeing
a ghostly figure of a woman . . . emerging nude from the surf,
only to vanish in the air before their eyes."*
—Haunted Indiana, *by Mark Marimen*

I had constraints enough in those other lives.
From the knob of Mt. Tom, I still shudder
at the faint corona of Chicago and how
for thirty-five years I burrowed through boxes
until, buried in a basement office, honing paragraphs
on astrophysics, I never viewed the stars. When I flung,
in 1915, the hour-glass meant to gauge an old maid's
waning time, I saw in the splinters a vision of shifting
sand and swirls of constellations. Byron's words:
"In Solitude . . . we are least alone," pierced
my insulated world like a gull's sharp cry.

                                         At first,
it was me, a blanket and some books, in a wilderness
where I slept in leeward swales and ate wild strawberries
from hillocks inching inland at the pace glaciers slide. But
that same summer a fisherman saw me skinny-dip
in the gray-lipped surf and, afterward, rumors grew:
how I was a dark-haired beauty, fleet-footed, who ran
with white-tailed deer and slept among the herd. Wives
had a different version: I was a siren who fled behind
foredunes to let myself be caught by any man
I could bewitch. The scent of marram grass
clung to their clothes.

                             In winter, when a wife steamed
the window of my shack with wrathful breath, I bought
a gun. Later, I took potshots at those who would snatch
my story for a byline. Byron's words held heavy irony

as I trudged steep slopes where sand absorbed my prints.

I was bathing in a kettle hole, a glacial pocket,
when the carpenter from LaPorte tracked me down. He pulled
the soiled clipping from his coat that told the world
Diana of the Dunes was Alice Mable Gray. He smoothed it
with his large hands as if it were a certificate to seal
our fate. That afternoon, we honeymooned
beneath the tamaracks and he vowed to guard the privacy
of our domestic bliss. While he fashioned furniture
from vines thick as his forearms, I sold boxes
of driftwood to those who couldn't believe how someone
so plain had been a legend.
           The first time he hit me, I understood—
after all, everyone pointed at him when a strangled
body washed up on our beach. *Indigents,* they called us,
but no one proved his guilt, and the beatings grew more severe.
He kept hemming in tighter and tighter the walks I took
and then moved us into town where I no longer heard
the breaking waves or that low hum shifting sands sing,
a bow drawn across taut strings.
           Ten years after seeking a hermitage,
I died in childbirth. The doctor who saw the bruises
wrote *complications* and drew up the sheet. No one noticed
that I was buried, not in the solitary plot my parents paid for,
but in a mass grave mixed with other bones. At least,
there was no box to burrow through, but clearly
I couldn't keep house with all those lost souls wringing
restless hands until resurrection morning.
           So I came back here,
to these sand-covered moraines where a glacier set down
its burden of debris. Having broken free
from society's strangle-hold, I am as resilient as the deer
who nuzzle me with kind eyes. *Solitude is an illusion,*

I whisper to children who suddenly fear the mound of sand others have pressed around them.

IV

The Grief of This World

"I sing his elegance with words that moan
and remember a sad breeze in the olive groves."
—Federico Garcia Lorca

I
A tongue takes for granted
the cherry stone of grief
that gravels the teeth—
the ruminating teeth—
the teeth that meet
with consternation
what does not yield
when pressed.

II
The grief of the world remains
like left-over pits on the plate
of a girl who cannot move
from her room until the eyes
of houses recede into sockets.
It is her hunger
that causes whatever there is,
to suffer. The trees loosen
their leaves when she brushes
her hair. The most innocent
implication stifles the songbirds.
A gesture can displace the route
of a breeze.

III
But what of the branches
bolted with harvest—peaches,
plums and cherries—muslin,
satin, silk? Even if they built themselves
into a bedstead the lush layers of mattress
would not restrain the shrewd seeds,
the seeds that snowball
through her sleep, seeds that sprout
a white avalanche of death, the impassive
tablecloth she stares at
while meadowlarks rise from the fields.

IV
The recognition jars me—
each time I hold my bright-eyed
daughter one last time before night
draws her beneath its foliage—
how branches relinquish
what they would clutch,
how the fruit braces its weight
against the air,
how life advances
toward perfection's pale stone.

V
In 1757, the gift of one ripe peach
pleasured a Delaware chief
so much that he spared
my ancestor the gauntlet.
The women washed away
his white blood
in the river and plucked
his beard until the skin was bald

as that pit he felt
below the ribs—
the core of loss
that would never leave him
though his dead wife
came to him in dreams
and his daughter spoke
in the gestures of village girls.

VI

The orchard. I always return
to the orchard. The way it was
the night before
when young people gathered
to slice and dry the apples
and then to congregate
beneath the trees, in the dark
promise
of a new moon.

VII

Morning, and only the cinders
of a house. The daughter stands
in a singed nightgown, her bald eyes
grasping the bough above her
and the peaches that strain toward what
she will never reach
before the stroke
brings her down.

VIII

In a book plate of Giorgione's
The Adoration of the Shepherds
Mary kneels serenely

near the feet of her infant Christ
while above her head a branch
bears the weight of something
burnt orange and bulging—
a cluster of mangos
with the features of faces.

Are they gargoyles
or are they angels? Are they buoyant
or are they brooding?
So much is hidden
by the mouth of the cave.

IX

Mary carries her child
into the room where the girl stares
at six left-over pits—
one for each month of a winter
held prisoner
inside a glass paperweight.

Mary shakes loose the snow
on the bulrushes and places her son
inside the vacuous basket
of arms. Afterwards,
the scent of lilies
lingers in the room.
The cherry stones are gone,
brushed discreetly
into the deep pocket of Mary's cloak.

X

As the One whom she adores
begins to eat the fruit upon the table,

the girl—who is now a woman—
washes his feet with what she sold
everything to buy.
She feels his grief and pleasure
in the way his hand touches
just once
the exuberance
of her hair.

XI

Nothing
but the linen cloth
she clutches
as she stumbles
through the cavern
and into the gaping mouth
that spits her
into the garden,

the burgeoning
garden, where a gardener
is tamping,
tamping the soil
of a sapling
that wasn't there
before. The air drips
with blossoms, it
thickens into a static
cascade
of sun and shadow
to dapple a face—any face—
turned toward
the woman.

And then he speaks her name
and she knows him—
the One bolted to the tree
who embraces sorrow
and lets it go
so that winter flows
into the hour of fruition,
so that the seeds of mortality
planted when we were born
grow into something
that dies
and rises from its death.

XII
Without touching
the man and woman
commence
the slow dance
of grief. Beneath
the lime trees
and the olive,
beneath the sky
and above the grass,
they sway
in that middle place,
we call an orchard,
that acre
that bears our love.

The Sunken Gardens

Huntington, Indiana
For my grandparents, Perry and Lucile Miller

> *Winding paths lead near cool waters and masses*
> *of bloom, in the place made out of a dream.*
> —Better Homes and Gardens, *Nov. 1929*

Poised on this limestone bridge, gray now,
but then it shone white, Lucile still wears
her bridal corsage, orchids pinned
to a stiff tailored suit. They have come,
like the others, to gaze into the cathedral
of their melded shadows where goldfish,
like shards of stained glass, glide. They marvel
at such beds of begonias and swirling
iris bordered by coleus. If paradise
can be designed from the raw gape
of a quarry, then the years can only add
their layers of bloom—cascading roses on Time's
great trellis. For the moment, at least,
they cannot foresee how this radiance
will fade, how negligence will mow
the flowers and vandals seize the rest.

Stone, water, grass . . . that's all
that will remain, the bare geometry
of a garden when memory has eroded its own
lush bank and they can't see beyond
the retaining wall somewhere in the thickening
mist, petunias so white they ache

in the moonlight. This pool has no bottom
but mud and more mud, but that can't be true,
and though you both wander through mazes
of beige hallways and can't reach each other
somewhere there must be a place, a chapel
freshly green where you meet. Maybe
it's here—on this bridge—where traffic is muffled
by maple leaves miles above what matters
in a life immortalized by the sudden
brush of a kiss.

The Pulley

On the path that loops the retirement village
my three-year-old could be my parent,
twenty years from now, wrapped to the neck
in an afghan and giving orders from a stroller
that might be a wheelchair—*the sun hurts my eyes,
I want to get out.* Each time
she speaks through her scarf, I pause
to bend down. Whose voice muffled through
years of wool do I hear? Perhaps it rises
from my own throat, far in the distance,
an old pulley groaning over its precarious
burden of water.

Teaching My Nephew
To See His Own Shadow

For Shea

"Look,
look at your shadow,"
I say but he
is gazing into
the sycamore
and smiling. "No,
it's here—
here in the grass."

It's late
afternoon
and our shadows
have stretched into
anorexic giants
searching
for food. I stoop
and touch
the ground
with his finger:
"This
is your shadow."

But already
he's scanning the air
as if tracking
a second shadow,
swift
as a hummingbird
tied to his wrist.

The Bears of Kalamazoo

My grandfather escaped from reunions
to photograph brown bears pacing
in and out of caves. Years later,
shaggy profiles interrupt games
of wiffle ball or Aunt Doris
stirring potato salad. "More bears,"
cousins groan when they spy
the familiar chain link fence
and plaster rocks. Inside
each blurred diamond is a bear
so small I could carry it
in my hand and blow on it, like dice,
for good luck. "Let's get to the people,"
my mother complains and the frames
click faster as if we're onboard
an accelerating train. My grandfather
slips into the fur coat of silence
he keeps near his chair. Already
he dreams the bears have crashed
through the fence and reached
the forest surrounding his home.
He opens the door but they wait
patiently in darkness that grows
vast as evening when he enters.

Working the Graves

The Choctaws tend their own
families first, so I go to older
hills near the back, break up
each plateau and then slope
the mounds on each side, the way
I've learned to hoe corn.

I take as my own, graves marked
by cedar or crepe myrtle and one
with a photo inside a locket—a woman
whose earrings are hammered
from tin.

Corine shakes loose sacks
of blue flowers while I wipe
the face of a ceramic Madonna
and Mr. Miles brags how Bessie,
his wife, could find short-cuts to church
through the swamp, snap off
the head of a snake.
At the last wake, he sat
in the back pew, explaining
why beans should be planted
on dark nights in April.

The sky is as bleached
as old limestone
when the teenagers arrive
in sports cars that spin gravel.
They linger by the gate, teasing
Rachel about a soldier she met
at the Satellite Disco. There's a rumor:
some deacons want to level
this land, hire a man to mow grass.

Germaine warns Marlena not to step
on the dead and for a moment there's
silence as we all watch our feet.
On slabs we poured and painted
last summer, black roses bleed
into "Infant, Slumbering Sweetly."

No one knows their names, not even
Old Man Carroll who, dressed
in his black suit and hat, pauses
at headstones as if they were doors
to houses on some remembered street.

Pisgah Road

September comes
and Amelia hears the music.
She moves one sore foot
at a time until her bones
crackle like burning sticks.

The hard clay hums
an afternoon song:
Come walk the road.
Come, one last time.

Amelia unwinds the rope
of her hair. It spreads
over her sunken
shoulders and breasts.
She finds the landmarks:
her birthplace, the dance ground,
her grandmother's grave
all hidden by briars.

In the scattered light
she stoops to gather
snakeroot and soft
clusters of mullein.

Her shadow runs on ahead.
It is thin and limber
and has bells on its feet.

Cedar Chest

Common sense would rule against
the cargo we keep inside its hold:
a wedding dress that will never fit again,
little league uniforms with grass stained
knees, baby shoes that jingle,
dried flowers no amount of water
will ever bring back. Unlikely
provisions for such a long voyage
when one day we haul up the anchor
and let the current take us where it may.

The Thief

They hear him in the attic
rummaging among boxes of clothes
they will never wear again.
While they're asleep, he sneaks
downstairs and steals linens
from the closet, stashes
chocolate cremes beneath his coat.
The old woman in our complex
claimed he was the landlord
and used his skeleton key to enter
while she was gone. She built
a maze of yard-sale furniture,
strung a clothesline the height
of his Adam's apple so he would
stumble in darkness he himself
created by snatching lightbulbs
from their sockets. Before he died
of starvation, my husband's grandfather
believed the culprit was a woman
who envied the only house
he ever owned. She mixed toxins
in the furniture polish and laced
his coffee with poison the policeman
assured was Coffee-mate. He had
to hide a baseball bat studded
with nails beneath his bed, but then
she boobie-trapped his mantel clock
so that it became a ticking bomb
at night. Miss Amelia who lived
in a chicken shack with a voodoo
cross above her bed, told me the thief
took everything but the jewels

she carried in a paper sack everywhere
she went. When she died, we discovered
nothing but a dimestore ring, the kind
a child might wear. A fortnight before
she was found inside her trailer,
a woman named Virginia, with extreme
arthritis and cataracts, gave me
a cardboard box of stories, unfinished
and written in pencil over the course
of forty years. "Keep them
and give them endings," she told me
as we snacked on saltine crackers
and sipped Hawaiian Punch from Dixie-cups.
"He's taken everything I have
but these—and now they're yours."

Convergence

I

This old building is a great ship,
and from the upper deck I watch
the moon each night cross
the window panes as if they
were calendar boxes.

The eastern sun splashes
our carpet's pink roses
and when the light pulls away,
it pulls away color,
until someday the roses will be
fainter than the color of flesh.

II

Three floors below in the hold,
a German woman dreams of her childhood
before the war—Albert Schweitzer,
a friend of her father's, performing
Bach in the parlor and long afternoons
sipping iced tea from hand-blown glass
that dazzled her eyes in the sun.

Now her windows are barred
portholes banked up with dirt,
none of her fixtures have light bulbs.
She sits in the television's watery blue
phosphorescence and when the glass falls
she can't find the pieces.

III

The wife of a Baptist preacher,
now deceased, tries to spray
away the odor of wet newspaper
seeping beneath the old woman's door.
During the day, she threads
mardigras beads into wind chimes,
ties them to pipes
that criss-cross her ceiling.

IV

We whisper in bed
as the woman we've never seen
runs her shower and we try
to remember the rooms
in our own childhood houses.

It's raining outside and the rain
is turning to ice.

V

Old Mr. Wilson who died soon after
last year's New Year's Eve party
climbs the spiraling staircase.

Lingering in the hallway, past four
in the morning, he clutched
a paper cup of champagne, described
the parking lot, how once it was
a croquet field with fountains
and goldfish that fed from his hands.

He's warning us of something
up ahead—half-hidden
in the dark water but rising
above our deck.

Tonight it will claim one of our own.

In his black, immaculate tuxedo,
the young violinist next door plays
"Jesu, Joy of Man's Desiring,"
while down below the wind chimes shake
like small chandeliers.

West Baden Springs Hotel
West Baden, Indiana

It's just a moment before Vesuvius,
and Mr. Sinclair stands erect beneath his opulent
dome, checking a gold pocket watch
one last time while Lillian's collie whines softly
at his feet, alert to some small sound, the shuffling
of cards or the opening of a car door, the chauffeur
pulling the chrome handle on Al Capone's
black Lincoln. It's before Capone steps out
and Joe Louis leaves to check-in on the side of town
where women who take in laundry toil
over lingerie edged with exquisite lace. Irving Berlin
whistles a snatch of what will be "Alexander's
Ragtime Band" as he pins a boutonniere
to his dapper lapel. The vendor, a girl
from French Lick, sees her violets wilt
in the sun that beats on the words, "Carlsbad
of America." Somewhere the click of dice,
someone wagers all he has that fate tips
her fan in his favor. But in the atrium,
stone muses are stoic, ready to take the rain
of dark ashes. Without shifting an eye,
they watch all that pass—the skirts that swish
and inch upward, the ruffles, plush hats, flirtatious
red feathers. A silent film star with insomnia
and female complaints presses her lips
to the rim of a glass and prays for the waters
to heal her. That's what they all ask,
though not in so many words. It's the hope
of the draw or the fear that their bluff
will be called, the glitter rub off in the wash. Lillian
falls asleep for hundreds of years and wakes

to find her husband a scoundrel as fake
as his spats. It's before she leaves with the soldier
who fought for breath in the trenches, before
her father dies and the collie lies buried
beneath the atrium floor. Vanderbilts
still stroll serene sawdust paths and silver
rings on crystal as John L. Sullivan cleans
his palate with pineapple sherbet. The milk-fed
capon sizzles in its broth. Electric lights blaze.

When the Market crashes, it's the collapse
of the cards; the guests fold what they have
and go home before gray flakes of silence
darken the dome, cover Apollo's Spring, fill
the Italianate fountain. The Jesuits come
with books and black robes to buy Pompeii
for a dollar.

Shoes

A German pianist three floors below me
stored sacks of shoes still in their boxes,
prices intact.
                    And when Miss Amelia died
in her two-room chicken shack, we found
new shoes forty years old—velvety ones
with black sequins, half a dozen
silver high heels—all in boxes so dusty
our fingers left prints.
                              Is it the dream
of a slipper suddenly turned crystal
that still lingers long after the knees
are too stiff to dance?
                              "Home," Dorothy said,
clicking her heels and an arthritic hand slides
from under the carpet, stretching for a wine glass
filled with rosé.
                        An old woman roams
through downtown, staring at mannequins,
at their beautiful shoes—buckles and flowers and
fluorescent laces. She forgets where she is—
is brought home by police.

When she takes off her brown penny loafers,
her feet are as white as the flesh of potatoes,
the calloused heels feel more and more
like scales on a fish.
                              Perhaps the old ones are looking
for shoes so tight they will never slip off
when the clock strikes twelve and they must run,
once again, down the long, spiraling staircase.

James Dean's Grave
Fairmount, Indiana

> *Forty acres of oats made a huge stage*
> *and when the audience left I took a nap*
> *and nothing got plowed or harrowed.*
> —Dean in an interview with Hedda Hopper

Where is the boy with bongo drums
and a matador's cape, with a fire-red motorcycle
racing through dust and fingers smeared
by chalk or clay?

He's not here.

He's not hovering over silk flowers and a stone
smack-full of rose-tinted kisses. He's not
fawning over cold cigarette butts or unfolding
love notes from strangers. He doesn't care
a hoot about staying where he's supposed to—lodged
among rows of graves and accessible to those
who chip and shove shards of headstone
into a purse.
     The boy who slept for years
with a piece of his mother's funeral wreath pressed
beneath his pillow would understand the need
to hold on to something, but those of you
who seek him—he's not here.

Better to fill your purses with chaff
for he's gone into the fields and if he's not
pounding ground with the beat
of rain, then he's riding wind hell-bent
over harrowed earth, stirring up dust. Or just

look for him in the solitary frame
of a farmer, shoulders slouched, hands
in his pockets, his worn boots scuffing
the crusted snow.

Benediction at Shore Cemetery

To John Mishler

When the cars have pulled away
and the green tent remains
like the last refrain of a hymn,
we stay to browse the unassuming
stones of ancestors who favored
the cultivated sod, the straight row.
You plowed as well as any
yet sought the wooded curve of creek
you slept with on nights in August
while water snakes and other mute
things that knew your language
purled the shallows near your head.
They called you "Silent Sam"
but my first memory of your voice
is how it shook the cows from the shadows
and brought them home through the dusk.
When we know of no good reason
to linger in this place bereft of benches,
only then comes the forlorn
cry of a kill-deer, plain-collared
plover of open fields with the pull
of ocean in its flight. It swings
and swoops above you, consecrating
the air, the grass, the sod—
your body in its dark sleep
entering the river.

Acknowledgments

Special thanks are offered to John Domont, www.domont-gallery.com, for permission to use his painting, "Moonrise, Indiana," copyright © John Domont, on the cover.

Grateful acknowledgment is made to the editors of the publications in which versions of many of these poems first appeared: *Artful Dodge, Arts Indiana Literary Supplement, Black Warrior Review, Christian Living, The Flying Island, Hopewell Review, Indiana Review, Indiannual 3, Maize, The Markle Times, The Mennonite, Mennonite Weekly Review, Midland Review, Poetry in Motion, Poetry On the Buses, Richland Community College Broadside Series, Southern Poetry Review, Zone 3*

"Family Tree" was nominated for a Pushcart Prize by *Artful Dodge.* "The Lighthouse Keeper's Wife" received Special Recognition in the Guy Owen Competition sponsored by *Southern Poetry Review.* "The Compound" received Juror's Choice in the Arts Council of Indianapolis Start with Art Competition. "Shoes" and "The Bears of Kalamazoo" won Honorable Mentions in the Chester Jones National Poetry Competition. "Covered Bridge" won first place in the Tipton Educational Center Poetry Contest. "The House of the Deaf Woman and the Belfry at Eragny" received Honorable Mention in the Write What You See Competition sponsored by the Writers' Center of Indianapolis and the Indianapolis Museum of Art.

Many of the poems in this book were written with fellowship assistance from the Arts Council of Indianapolis with the support of the Ruth Lilly Trust and the Lilly Endowment and from the Indiana Arts Commission with the support of The National Endowment for the Arts.

The Author

Shari Miller Wagner was born in Goshen, Indiana, but grew up near the small town of Markle. During her eighth grade year, her family moved to Somalia where her father worked at a Mennonite mission hospital while she and her sister attended a boarding school near Nairobi.

After graduating from Goshen College, Shari worked for two years under a service agency of the Mennonite Church, helping the Clifton-Choctaw of Louisiana research its history for Federal Recognition.

Shari holds an M.F.A. in Creative Writing from Indiana University and has taught writing in universities, elementary schools and nursing homes. She has received several fellowships from the Arts Council of Indianapolis and the Indiana Arts Commission, and her poetry has appeared in *Indiana Review, Black Warrior Review, Midland Review, Southern Poetry Review,* and in the anthology, *A Cappella: Mennonite Voices in Poetry.*

She currently is editor of *MennoExpressions,* a publication of First Mennonite Church of Indianapolis and lives with her husband, Chuck, and their two daughters, Vienna and Iona, in Westfield, Indiana.

Printed in the United States
36356LVS00002B/7-21

9 781931 038294